Forthcoming from Upptäcka Press

Also in this series by Geoff Hall:

The Cultural Way of Being

Translating the Invisible Wind

The Artist's Autobiography

By Chris Lorensson

Slurp, Gulp and start on Sounds

Mirror

Tricks of Postmodern Urbanism

Geoff Hall

The Wilderness and the Desert of the Real

Part 1 of 4 in

Spiritual Direction in a Postmodern Landscape

Edited by Chris Lorensson

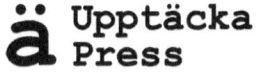 Upptäcka Press

First printing in 2011. This 1ˢᵗ edition published 2011 by Upptäcka Press.

Upptäcka Press publishes 'Unorthodox thoughts on Christian Spirituality'. Originally spawned from the international writer's collaborative *Upptäcka Network* (upptacka.net, founded 2005), Upptäcka Press strives to develop and distribute works which illuminate post-modern thought in a spiritual context using any media necessary.

Upptäcka Press
7 Dalrymple Rd
Bristol BS2 8YJ
England, UK

upptacka.com
info@upptacka.com
on Twitter @upptacka

Liberation typeface originally designed by Steve Matteson, © Ascender Corp.

Cover photograph by © 2010 Mark Hall. Design & layout by LorenssonDesign&Co. (lorensson.co.uk)

ISBN 978-0-9568034-0-5

Join the conversation at **PostmodernLandscape.com**

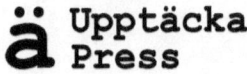

Contents

To Jeanette, for her love and patience

Introduction from the author

Four books, four different map coordinates. Starting with our calling in the arts and what this will mean for our lives, we move on to how we will have a cultural impact in our work. 'The Cultural Way of Being' reveals that it is in community and not isolation, that our work will flourish. The farther we look back, the more we see of the future landscape. 'Translating the Invisible Wind' gets to the heart of an art free from Institutional burdens and the demand for our collaboration to produce propaganda. Finally, we rest at the oasis of knowing ourselves, the 'Autobiography' will give us the tools we need to understand who we are and what we are doing on this beautiful planet with its diverse cultural terrains.

The landscape travelled in 2011 will reinforce the calling of the artist to be culturally formative, transforming the Postmodern landscape with hope pregnant with anticipation as we celebrate the epistemology of love.

This exploration of redemption's landscape will equip the artist with the freedom to explore the pressing issues of our day. If we're to have a cultural impact and see renewal, it is essential that we transform the lot of the artist.

We need to share our lives together in community. It starts today.

I wish the world was flat like the old days
Then I could travel just by folding a map
No more airplanes, or speed trains, or freeways
There'd be no distance that could hold us back.

'The New Year', Death Cab for Cutie

Cast of Characters

There are two deserts: the *personal testing ground* and the philosophically proclaimed *Desert of the Real*. Not all experiences of the former are uni-form, standardised treks on the desert terrain. (The five spiritual laws of trekking?)

Moses had a family and his sojourn lasted 40 years—only to return to the same place years later and receive the Law.

David was with a band of outlawed men and women, roaming the desert places to escape the tyranny of a wayward king.

Elijah—after delivering the news of an impending drought—was told to escape to the Kerith Ravine, where he is fed by the Ravens! The river dries up because of the drought and he moves on.

Jesus was directed to the desert by the Spirit, where He spent 40 days and nights. He was tempted by the devil on three points: provision, protection and false worship. Jesus rejects the temptation and the antagonist leaves. Before He leaves the wilderness His needs are ministered to by angels.

Paul, we believe, having received the Call, ended up in the wilderness of Arabia for around 3 years. There is no information about the details of this, but by piecing together time scales which Paul talks about in his letters, it may be the place where he received the vision of *Paradise and the Seventh Heaven* ('whether in the body or out of the body').

The Wilderness of Sin?

How can we understand this sojourn in the wilderness?
Simply put—between *the Call* and *its realisation*, comes
The Wilderness!

Much faith is lost during these times of attrition because there is no-one to guide us through such experiences. We crave security and abundant provision—not The Desert life. Our churches are spiritually polluted by their view of *righteousness = prosperity.* The guides of prosperity divert the call of God into their own service, rather than guiding those who are called as artists to go through The Wilderness. The Wilderness = sin! Much of the work of God in Creation is lost because of this diversion of talent. We reside in The Desert to find out about who we are; precious, beloved and born of God. Faith is stillborn; gifts are rendered redundant by a Church which needs to be fed and doesn't want too many of its congregation going through times of attrition. (Think of the financial repercussions!)

Our personal wilderness prepares us for the terrain of The Postmodern Desert of the Real. This Wilderness is not the experience of the *absence* of God, but of the presence of God in a difficult landscape. It has been called 'Practicing the Presence of God' by some. I want us to think of it as 'Embodying the Presence of God'. I want to apply this to the journey of the artist because this experience creates a depth of character, vision and awareness which will inform our work in the arts.

> *I believe that it is always through spiritual crisis that healing occurs. A spiritual crisis is an attempt to find oneself, to acquire new faith. It is the apportioned lot of everyone whose objectives are on the spiritual plane. And how could it be otherwise when the soul yearns for harmony, and life is full of discordance. This dichotomy is the stimulus for movement, the source at once of our pain and of our hope; confirmation of our spiritual depths and potential.* [1]

Jesus was tested on the provision of food, on protection from harm and finally, with power over the nations if He should succumb to 'a little idolatry'. As for the latter, it was not the devil's to give, as *the Earth is the Lord's.* We will be tested in similar ways.

1. Andrei Tarkovsky. 'Sculpting in Time.' Translated by Kitty Hunter-Blair. Published by University of Texas Press, 1987. p.193.

Direction through a Weary Land

Our compass direction is set to 'North'. This is not *towards* God—God is already present with us—but it is more from The Wilderness to cultivated land, from a hidden, obscure life, to a public life. It is the transition between the two which we find the trickiest!

If God is drawing us from public life to a hidden life, this is not rejection, but transformation and renewal—not sin, but grace and healing at work. The Wilderness experience is not part of a linear progression, a simple 'from/to' story, where every issue is resolved and personal foibles corrected. God doesn't desire automatons, but wants us to live in the freedom bought for us. God desires us to freely give a response of love and adoration.

Spirituality isn't something practiced in times of attrition, but embodied in every experience of life and creativity.

Spirituality is not something additional—an optional extra which we apply to our professional lives when we suspect the superficiality of our self-driven endeavours—it is a matter of being, of who we are. Remember, our spirituality may be directed, mis-directed or re-directed. We therefore need the counsel and guidance of those who have walked the desert track-ways and know the terrain.

The Wilderness is a Place of Intimacy

Henri Nouwen, in his book 'Adam, God's Beloved' wrote about this hidden life:

> ...just after His baptism, Jesus was led by the Spirit into the Wilderness for forty days where He was tempted by the devil. The desert in the spiritual life, is the place of temptation, trial and purification. [2]

I would add to this, that it is (strangely) also a place of healing through crisis, a time of recuperation and an intimate landscape as evinced in the life of Elijah. He was sustained with water from a brook and food from the Ravens. He not only prophesied the drought, but he lived it!

On another occasion, after a death-threat, he fled into the wilderness and whilst sleeping, was disturbed by an angel who provided food and drink to aid in his recovery from the arduous journey. After he had rested, he went farther into the wilderness, found a cave and rested again. When he arrives at the cave he is told to climb to the top of the mountain, where finally he hears a 'still small voice'. He is directed to go back through the

2. Henri Nouwen, published by Darton, Longman and Todd. 1997. p.21.

desert track-ways in the South of the country, heading North to Damascus.

If we followed this on a map it may look like the meaningless meandering of a desperate man trying to evade the murderous intent of the authorities; unless we had the intimate knowledge of his conversations with God. Maps may show our location, but they do not record spiritual intimacy. They do not reveal the secret, quiet, sacred conversations we have with God!

Why is this hidden life so important for an artist?

At Work in the Digital Babel

Outside of The Wilderness we're bombarded with messages encouraging us to self-realise, self-actualise, self-promote: *we are what we achieve, what we possess, what we control!* We are the sum-total of our power to consume! When God removes us from the throng of this civilisation and plants us in an alien landscape, it's so we hear the 'still, small voice'.

The Wilderness journey is at the very core of the 'cultural way of being' [3]; it is the only thing which grounds us in the spiritual life of the artist and helps orientate ourselves in the coming Desert of the Real.

There is no prescription for this journey. There are no 'five spiritual laws' or 'ten commandments' for this spiritual life, nor is there a designated route to take when negotiating the transition.

Transition: from Personal Salvation to Saving Society at Large

For Elijah it was, in part, a route he'd already taken to his secret meeting with God. Jesus was led into the wilderness and needed the ministry of angels to help Him out again.

3. Part 2 of 4 in this series, forthcoming.

There is no strict time-frame for this journey. We are dependent on the Spirit of God to direct, to prompt, to hold us in one place or another. It's not a logical transition. What we learn from the exemplars cited above is that they knew where their re-integration was to occur.

What The Wilderness teaches us is to listen for the voice of God—the still, small voice—to discern it from the earthquake, wind and fire. On re-entering the public life there is a cacophony of noise which can drown out that voice. The Desert of the Real is a culture of disquiet which can disorientate our lives and creative gifts.

Postmodern Carnivals

If in The Desert of the Real we begin looking at the carnival side-shows for clues showing us where to participate; our gaze is distracted. The urge is for one of acceptance—to blend in, to find our guiding direction culturally by the phenomena around us because we don't know who we are or what we are here for.

The Wilderness experience will teach us these two main factors: *who we are* and *what we are here for* – our calling. The art we make—whether, word, image or performance art—will communicate incoherence if these things are not well-developed in our hearts. If we're ignorant about how much we are loved and are unable to resolve that crisis within, we will not resolve it in our art. All we will produce is another consumer item. The Wilderness, in all its harsh reality, teaches us the gift of love.

The *transition* is a crossroads in our lives:

> It seems to me that the individual today stands at a crossroads,
> faced with the choice of whether to pursue the existence of
> a blind consumer, subject to the implacable march of new
> technology and the endless multiplication of material goods,
> or to seek out a way that will lead to spiritual responsibility,
> a way that ultimately might mean not only [their] personal
> salvation, but also the saving of society at large; in other
> words, to turn to God...That is the step which becomes
> a sacrifice, in the Christian sense of self-sacrifice. [4]

Robert Bresson, the great French filmmaker, wrote 'Translate the invisible wind by the water it sculpts in passing.' Our work as artists is to discern that movement. Whilst the wind 'blows wherever it will', we are to be sensitive to that movement and then translate it into something others can see, hear or perceive. This is the art of perception, and not of consumption.

4. ibid, p.218

The Desert of the Real

From the wilderness, Jesus returned to Galilee, moving house from Nazareth to a lakeside apartment in Capernaum. In public he echoed the words of John the Baptist, reiterating the message that things in Israel were going to change; a new order was arising.

Elijah went to Damascus to anoint two new kings. He is given an assistant, Elisha, who succeeds him in his work of *disturbing the comfortable.*

As we consider this for ourselves (our entrance into public life), we should now look at The Postmodern Desert.

Baudrillard writes this about The Desert of the Real,

Abstraction today is no longer that of the map, the double, the mirror or the concept. Simulation is no longer that of a territory, a referential being or a substance. It is the generation by models of a real without origin or reality: a hyperreal. The territory no longer precedes the map, nor survives it. Henceforth, it is the map that precedes the territory - precession of simulacra - it is the map that engenders the territory and if we were to revive the fable today, it would be the territory whose shreds are slowly rotting across the map. It is the real, and not the map, whose vestiges subsist here and there, in the deserts which are no longer those of the Empire, but our own. The desert of the real itself...It is a hyperreal: the product of an irradiating synthesis of combinatory models in a hyperspace without atmosphere. [5]

There is a sense of sophistry in much of Postmodern philosophical writing meant to unsettle and disorientate us.

Olson writes about Baudrillard's world, his Desert of the Real. You will see the similarities to The Wilderness experience, i.e. the seeming lack of referentials, but beyond that they are mere ethereal shadows passing with the movement of the sun and clouds.

5. Jean Baudrillard. 'Simulacra and Simulation'. Translated by Sheila Faria Glaser. Published by The University of Michigan Press. 1994. p1&2

Baudrillard...finds himself within a simulacra, an era of
simulation, which suggests for him a time in which all
referentials have been liquidated. This artificial, malleable
time that leans towards equivalence represents faking
that which one does not possess, suggesting an absence
rather than a presence and threatening the distinction
between true and false, real and imaginary. [6]

For Baudrillard, the reality of 'apocalypse forever' limits apocalypse to disaster and does not consider revelation and redemption. This is his dark terrain—The Desert of the Real. As Lyon points out,

Ecological disaster, moral panic in the wake of
AIDS, these represent the abyss beyond which, for
Baudrillard...no redemptive moment lies. [7]

Buddhist Nihilism

Tied with this despair is the nihilism of Postmodernism; in many Postmodern thinkers we find a synthesis with Buddhism's Philosophy of Life.

6. Carl Olson. 'Zen and the Art of Postmodern Philosophy'. Published by State University of New York Press. 2000, p208
7. David Lyon. 'Postmodernity'. Published by Open University Press, 1994. p.73

In the Buddhist Mahāyāna poetry of Nagarjuna, what we see is a lengthened negative parallelism within a stanza. It posits a thing only in the next trope to deny its existence.

Difference is not in a different thing.
Nor is it in a non-different thing.

If difference does not exist,
Neither different nor identical things exist. [8]

To aid our comparison of the difference between this worldview and one based on Scriptural wisdom, let's look at the poetry of Job.

Behold I go forward but he is not there,
And backward, but I cannot perceive Him;
When he acts on the left, I cannot behold him;
He turns on the right, I cannot see Him.
(But He knows the way I take,
When He has tried me, I shall come forth as gold.) [9]

This is a simple example employing opposing directions as well as different ways of knowing God: perception, beholding and physical seeing. Throughout The Book of Job we have complex poetic parallelisms in which the first line is playfully answered

8. Nagarjuna. 'The Fundamental Wisdom of the Middle Way.' (Nagarjuna's Mūlamadhyamakakārikā) Translated by Jay L Garfield. Published by Oxford University Press, 1995. p38
9. Job chapter 23, verses 8-10. NASV

by the second. (Some of this rich nuance has, I fear, been lost in translation.) This sense of direction employed by the writer/poet is pertinent to our sojourn in The Wilderness. Many times we will feel like Job. However, the end of that section doesn't see him giving up the hope of redemption, but reinforcing it. Job may have lost track of God in his Wilderness, but God has not lost track of him! Tried and tested in the heat of the desert furnace, he will become like purified gold.

Embracing the Buddha

Any embrace of Buddhist philosophy and worldview has to be shunned because at the core is the great *'nihil'*, nothingness. Our resistance consists of denying nihilism a hold on our lives by refuting it as a guiding light. It is a reverse logic or reasoning—a celebration of anti-life. What then of Buddhist Art? Is there not a tension between the unconfessed belief in the *nihil* and the beautifully crafted artwork and architecture? Is this what the Buddha had in-mind? Such art appears to be the ultimate in anti-art and not Duchamp's concept of the 'found-object'!

Synthetic Spirituality

The Desert of the Real—a simulacrum of non-existence—
reveals a synthesis between Buddhist and Postmodern thought:
being and non-being, real and imaginary, or even reality
and hyperreality.

We don't have to believe in it, we just have to be incredulous to
it so that we break its spell over our hearts and minds. To believe
it is to believe a delusion. This illusory thread takes us back
to John's Apocalyptic Poem, written during a time of powerful
delusion, wherein people are dazzled and deceived by inanimate
images! This ancient thread has not been erased and is still
present today. In considering the human condition, we must also
consider human conditioning.

Mimicking Mayhem

Whilst caught in the web of contemporary delusions we end up
creating work which mimics the side-shows in the postmodern
carnival; aping the 'norms' and forms in The Desert of the Real.
Do we seek illusory relevance or an authenticity which leads
to credibility? If we choose relevance, then we become mere

mimics. If we choose authenticity, then we become creators of imaginative landscapes through which others can travel. Our concern is creating future landscapes, not attempting to follow the wind of fleeting trends in the *here and now.* We generate the possibility of redemption, we do not add to Postmodern turbulence.

Prophetic Imagination

Walter Brueggemann in his marvellous book, 'The Prophetic Imagination' calls for this intent in our life together,

> *I am urging...that if the church is to be faithful it must be formed and ordered from the inside of its experience and confession and not by borrowing from sources external to its own life.* [10]

I am also urging this to be the case for artistry with a radical Christian spirituality. We therefore need to shun all attempts to synthesise from outside our experience and confession, but also from control within it.

The artist wants to get to the marketplace to participate in the conversation. The theologian wants to control the conversation. The artist wants a free-forming discourse on the plastic horizon. The theologian wants to measure the distance to the horizon and make sure nobody goes beyond it.

10. Walter Brueggemann. Published by Fortress Press, 2001. p5

Theology through the arts is problematic in that *art is not theology,* and if the flow reverses the other way, you end up doing the arts *through* theology! Artistic language is aesthetic—not theological—for once theological language is applied to the creation of art you end up with tired symbolism; the art of ecclesiastical propaganda! (The code of another simulacrum?)

In The Desert of the Real we have no need to walk alone. There are guides here who can help with Spiritual Direction in a Postmodern Landscape. If we come through our sojourn in The Wilderness we are not only tried and tested, but refined. This is preparation for The Desert of the Real, or perhaps we should now declare it as The Desert of the *un*Real, where the temptation is not to reach the nearest oasis, but of heading off towards the mirage.

With the songwriter of the wonderfully named Song #17, this is our attitude of heart:

> *I'm not trying to get my way*
> *in the world's way.*
> *I'm trying to get your way,*
> *your Word's way.*
> *I'm staying on your trail;*
> *I'm putting one foot*
> *In front of the other*
> *I'm not giving up.*

Also in the series *Spiritual Direction in a Postmodern Landscape*

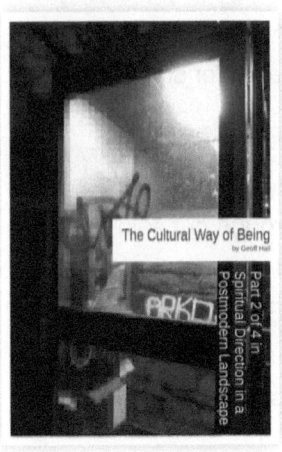

The Cultural Way of Being

Part 2 of 4

This book offers encouragement to those who want to know how their work can become culturally formative and not just personally expressive. The Cultural Way of Being is rooted in 21st Century culture and calls for artists to shun cultural evacuation and resurrect spirituality.

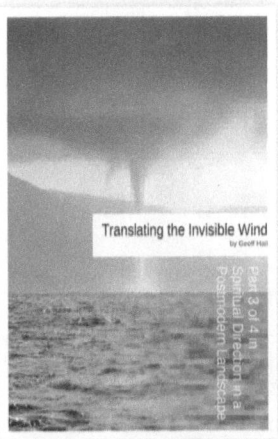

Translating the Invisible Wind

Part 3 of 4

Translate calls the artist to reject institutional subservience and form part of a living artistic community. Jacques Ellul warns us that if we pursue the methods of propaganda, we will become like any other ideology and lose the essence of our faith. Do we collaborate with the powerful? Can we resist the temptation to conform to the spirit of the age, so that we can transform a fractured, disintegrated culture?

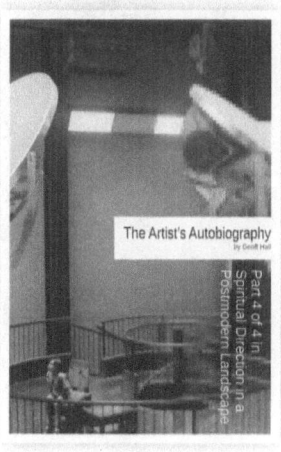

The Artist's Autobiography

The Artist's Autobiography

Part 4 of 4

One of the biggest issues I'm asked about in my capacity as an arts mentor focuses on identity. "Who am I as an artist?" The next serious question is then "How should my faith inform and give shape to my work?" Autobiography will help artists to grapple with the issues from within redemption's story and guide them to find a place to live and work in contemporary culture.

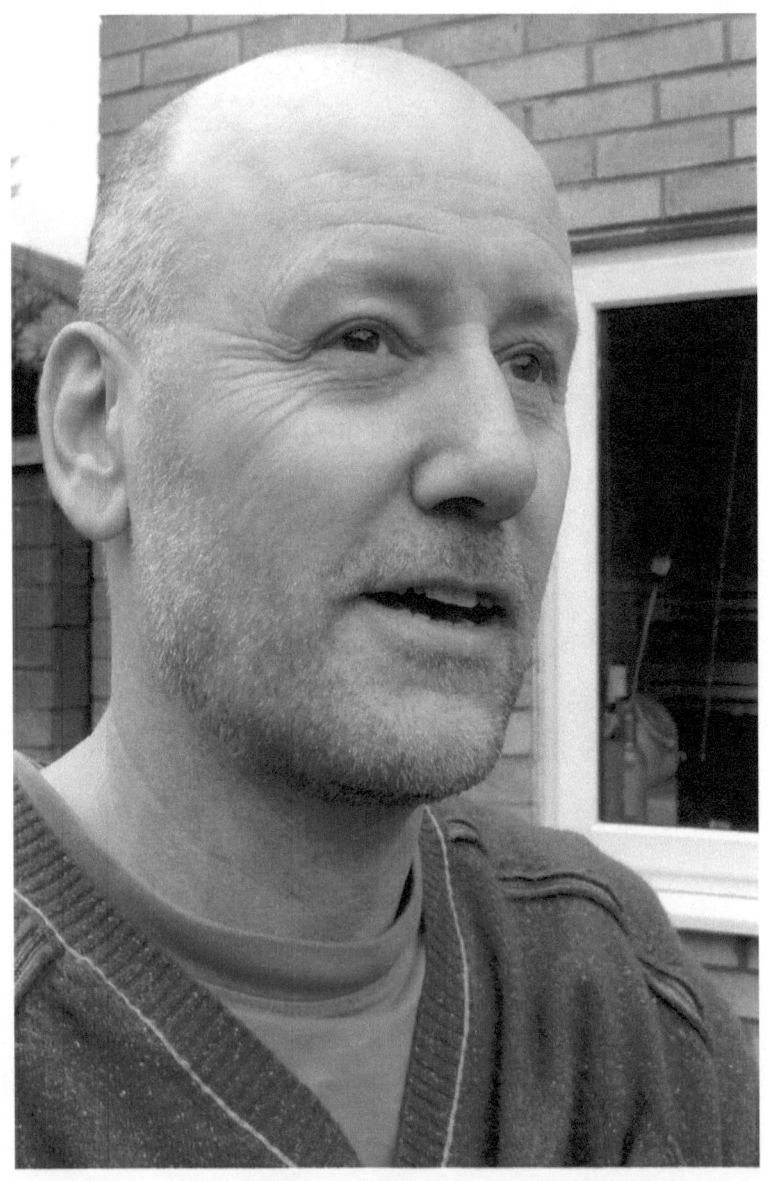

About the author

Born in 1957, Geoff lived for the next 30 years in the tight-knit community of Hartlepool in the North-East of England. At the age of 16 Geoff left an unremarkable time at school and became an electrician.

In the early 1980's—two years after completing his apprenticeship—he was made redundant and never worked as an 'sparky' again. (Geoff is from a working-class background and for those reading this in the States, class is a similar divide in the UK as 'race' is in America. Despite this social and economic 'disadvantage' Geoff was part of a great extended family). His parents worked hard to keep the family together. His Dad was a great footballer and often took Geoff up to the local recreation ground for a little coaching. Inevitably it seemed that these sessions turned into great social occasions, with a coached 11 a-side football game. After such events I remember there were knocks on our front door, asking if 'Mr Hall' was coming out to play.

During those days of recession and unemployment, two significant people entered Geoff's life, Richard and Janice Russell. Richard had entered a Curacy at a local church and Janice was a painter of great aesthetic sensitivity and expression. Geoff doesn't know how these things happened, but Richard saw in him 'potential'. (Now it should be said that this word was on Geoff's 'most-hated words' list, as many had said to him that he had great "potential"), but it felt like a curse, as it was never realised! Richard started passing books to him on philosophy, Kant's 'Critique of Judgement' and Hegel's 'Aesthetiks'. Discussions followed and Richard then gave Geoff Calvin Seerveld's 'Rainbows for a Fallen World', Hans Rookmaaker's 'Modern Art and the Death of a Culture', along with the heavy tome, Herman Dooyeweerd's grand opus 'A New Critique of Theoretical Thought'. (Now remember, this is an unemployed electrician from Hartlepool, who barely scraped through school.)

The art of learning and personal development is seeing potential in someone *and then doing something about it*. Without this intervention, what was going to be an unremarkable life of frustration and unrealised potential, Geoff's life was turned around by these two amazing people with a great loving and transformational spirit. By the time Richard and Janice left Hartlepool to move to Bath the seeds had been sewn.

Geoff went from one contract job to another and during a time of long-term unemployment delivered telephone directories to homes in the North-East of England to get a little Christmas money. In those days Hartlepool had an unemployment rate of +25%! During his last contract Geoff looked for a change of direction which led him to study for a degree in Bristol. In 1987, Geoff. his wife and 18 month old son left their home in

Hartlepool and headed south, where Geoff majored in Art History at Bristol Polytechnic.

After graduation in 1990, Geoff worked with the Royal Commission of Historical Monuments of England as a photographic curator for the next 15 years, whilst also undertaking a Post Graduate degree at Exeter where his research focused on developing a cultural narrative for the National Curriculum for Art.

In 2005, Geoff was made redundant, which would then happen twice again at City of Bristol College, (working as a tutor) and Saint Stephens Church, where he worked as an Arts Development Officer.

After a meeting with Tim Woodford and Ben Small, they embarked on the creation of a film company, Handy Cloud Productions. In 2009, the first Handy Cloud film was produced, "ONE", which was taken to Los Angeles where it received 'critical acclaim' after its showing at the Alex Theatre in Glendale. The company continues to look for opportunities to make more films for TV and Cinema.

Towards the end of 2010, his heart firmly set on using his gifts to 'make a difference', Geoff was approached by Chris Lorensson of Upptäcka Press about publishing some of his writing and developing the ArtsMentoring.Co business. They are thrilled to be able to see the fruits of this new adventure with a series of books on 'Spiritual Direction in a Postmodern Landscape'.

As a writer

By the age of 8 I had fended off three death-threatening episodes, involving a dummy (soother), a van and a motorbike. It was not my intent to embark on a thrill-seeking journey through life, but having conquered my fear of death and seeing something of the 'other side', I continued to have numerous accidents, including my most recent, falling off a train at Bristol Parkway train station. I live, still, near the Station which almost claimed my life and where I disappointed the attending Ambulance crew, who wanted to collect body parts from under the train. More exciting…apparently!

In my writing I continue to wrestle with the ghosts of Bresson, Bergman, Kieslowski and Tarkovsky as I seek to understand more of our spiritual condition and its many socio-cultural incarnations. My primary concerns are creating the depth of character for an actor to play with and the aesthetics of the cinematic/iconic.

Tired of films about British working class families with a predilection in the characters towards criminal violence and eschewing the desperation of period dramas as a metaphor for goodness knows what, I seek to express a different nuance of contemporary (European) life, blended with the spirituality of the aforementioned ghosts.

I am endeavouring to create a style of filmmaking called 'cinema in extremis', a poetic style of storytelling which focuses on characters who are at a point in their lives of either breaking, or finding redemption.

A brief history

I started mentoring in 2001, after a student at my church was told that 'her faith was inappropriate for a student at their college'. After talking at a meeting at the college in question, I found that there were others who had suffered the same kind of abuse. Whilst thinking I could limit myself to cerebral, even spiritual things on her behalf, I decided that personal commitment was needed. A monthly meeting was set up to provide encouragement and cultural critique, as well as giving the artists a space to talk about their work and have an 'open critique'.

Over the years The Group, so ably named by imaginative, creative people (!), has grown to over 60 artists around Bristol and the South West. The original focus on visual artists has expanded to include word, image and performance arts. We have at times been courted by local institutions of spirituality and education, but the glue has never been strong enough to stick for any length of time and we are now free again from bureaucracy! We do not it seems, fit well into institutionalised forms of spirituality, because in the end they can never resist the urge to control what is happening. Spiritual consumerism and not community building, becomes the guiding hand on all things.

In 2007, we put on an exhibition entitled 'Set All Free' at our local gallery – Grant Bradley – which included painting, sculpture, installation (including video), ceramics, photography and poetry. We had a gospel choir for the Preview, which had an impact on the proprietors; the place packed out for a wonderful show.

Between 2007 and 2009, 'The Tree House', a monthly café event, gave space for dance, fashion producers showing their work, film, performance poetry, cultural critique, a philosopher's corner and talks on visual art, plus live music. We met for 2 years in Saint Stephens Café, in the Heart o' the City of Bristol! We are looking to revisit those nights at another venue.

My journey is as someone involved in the arts from an early age, including as a child playing the drums on a biscuit-tin - for our living-room band - to 60's pop songs. Alas, it didn't last long! I thought I was destined to be a songwriter, but I was wrong. The final nail in the coffin came when my local church would only support me if I became a worship leader - obviously minus the biscuit-tin! The thought of this shooked me to the core. I didn't want to play or write church music, but wanted to get 'out there' and be part of the rich conversation.

In the late 80's we moved to Bristol to effect a change of direction. I studied at Bristol Polytechnic and majored in Art History. My dissertation was on the 'Iconoclastic Disorders of the 16th Century'. In the 90's whilst holding down a job as a photographic curator, I studied for a research degree at the

University of Exeter, for which I received an MPhil. A great disappointment to me, because I'd wanted a PhD, but if you write about new ways of developing the art curriculum along narrative lines, then you ask for it from the protectors of the status quo. It was controversial, so bite me! Never one for a quiet life, never one for following the established pathways and maintaining the status quo, is who I am. You don't always get what you want, of course! Sometimes you have to deal with personal disappointment and sometimes the disappointment of others.

I'm inspired by people like Dietrich Bonhoeffer, who was part of the resistance to the Nazi Regime in Germany and also Jacques Ellul a writer of great insight and spirituality and a member of the French Resistance. Yes, you may perceive a thread there in my choice of heroes! Resistance is never futile!

My experience of church has led me to feel unwelcome there; save for friendships I'd probably not go. My problem concerns worldview and language, each supporting the other in the retreat of christian spirituality into the self-constructed ghetto of the sub-culture. I'm sure what we have today is not what Jesus had in mind. When I see the response to his institutional days, attending and speaking at Synagogue, I am confronted by the murderous intent of those who rejected his teaching. His move to the highways and byways showed a different kind of communication, the story of everyday life, the parable form. We tend to use the language of the synagogue in such public spaces and wonder why people don't respond to our invitation.

The reflex of the Church to control everything under its roof, leads to the distortion of the arts. They can no longer function as free-forming material on the plastic horizon, but are reshaped by theological & ecclesiastical language and concerns. The Reformation set the artist free from ecclesiastical servitude. Once emancipated, it is best not to appeal to your former gaolers for a bed for the night. You may be there for much longer. It's not all black & white of course, but this is my experience so far. Oh, for a wind of change!

So, this is me. Part writer, part mentor. I've a heart for people and 'things', the 'things' which Jesus concerns Himself about, everyday life, everyday creativity, as well as everyday people. In the Postmodern landscape of fractured lives and fractured things, we need to walk together, not stand alone.

Geoff Hall. Bristol, UK. 2010, ArtsMentoring.Co

Join the conversation

PostmodernLandscape.com

Share your thoughts about this book and read what others have to say in comments and the forum.

HandyCloud.com

Geoff and Tim Woodford's film production house where the critically-acclaimed film *ONE* was debuted at the famous Alex Theatre in Glendale, California.

ArtsMentoring.Co

visit Geoff's artist mentoring website for articles along the same lines of thought in this series of books.

Reference

This book is written to introduce the terrain of Spiritual Direction to the artist, with its evocation of imaginative spaces in which to meditate on the cultural situation before us. If we learn from the hardships of The Wilderness, this will prepare us for the Desert of the Real.

The Wilderness challenges our resolve to follow an artistic life with its lack of resources and is a proving ground for our integrity as artists. The Desert of the Real offers the opposite of this experience, with its abundance of distractions, each calling us to respond and create a 'relevant' (but perhaps synthetic) art.

In the pages of this book I've offered these two scenarios for your contemplation. Use this notebook to record your thoughts or questions, and please do share with us at Upptacka.com Let's get talking with one another!